COVERED

Living In Triumph While

Going Through Trials

On A Deeper Level

Jackie Dighans

Covered Bonus Material

COVERED Living In Triumph While Going Through Trials On A Deeper Level
Publisher of Peace
Miles City, Montana

ISBN: 979-8-9877483-0-5

Library of Congress Control Number: 2023902831

Cover and interior design by: Sabrina Wages
Editing by: Sabrina Wages
Illustrations by: Rayne Idland Photography and Photos by Kristy

Table of Contents

Suggestions on How to Use this Bonus Material

- This booklet was created to accompany the book COVERED Living in triumph while going through trials.
- Use it as a personal study guide in your own time with the Lord to go deeper in Him.
- Use it in a group study. Everyone having their own book and bonus material booklet.
  - Do it as an 8-week study and just touch the surface of this transformational study together.
  - Do it as a 16-week study and go more in depth as a group.
  - Whatever you choose there are enough questions to do some together and some for your personal study.
- Get creative and do what works best for your personal time or group.
- The most important thing is that you and each one in your group grow and go to the next level in your walk of faith.
- If you find you want to get more serious about your growth and want to work with me one on one or in a group, contact me and we will make a plan that will work and get you the results you are desiring. Jackiedighans@gmail.com
- Join COVERED Group Coaching - email me for details.
- Also look at Author's Services in the back of this book.
- Enjoy the journey.

Introduction

1. James 1:2-4
   Meditate on these verses. How can you start walking in them today?

   _____

   _____

2. What if your past, if you hold the right mindset around it, can propel
   you to the prize of the high call of God? How would that affect
   your life?

   _____

   _____

   _____

3. What if all the circumstances you are walking through are preparing
   you for God's purpose for you? How does this change your outlook?

   _____

   _____

   _____

   _____

4. What if the way you go through life is the most important lesson?
   What would that lesson mean to you?

   _____

   _____

   _____

5. What are you allowing to be produced in you as you walk through circumstances?

_____

_____

_____

6. What would change if you decided to do what this Word (James 1:2-4) advises?

_____

_____

_____

_____

7. What could your life look like if you consider it a joy, even pure joy, when trials come? Is that unimaginable?

_____

_____

_____

_____

8. What are you going to let your trials produce in you as a child of God?

_____

_____

_____

9. Are you able to decide you won't let them move or shake you? How would this change you?

_____

_____

10. What if you let trials do their work in you and make you mature and complete, lacking nothing? What does this mean to you?

_____

_____

_____

_____

11. Are you able to hold a perspective of "What can I learn through these trials?

_____

_____

_____

_____

12. How do you personally want to go through hard times?

_____

_____

_____

_____

13. What results do you want; Growth and Maturity or Stuck and Lukewarm? Why?

_____

_____

_____

_____

COVERED

_____

_____

_____

_____

_____

_____

_____

_____

_____

_____

_____

_____

_____

_____

_____

_____

_____

_____

_____

_____

_____

ON A DEEPER LEVEL

_____

_____

_____

_____

_____

_____

_____

_____

_____

_____

_____

_____

_____

_____

_____

_____

_____

_____

_____

_____

_____

_____

_____

_____

Chapter 1

I Thought We Didn't Believe In That...

1. What surprises (circumstances/situations) came up for you as a child?

_____

_____

_____

2. Did any scenarios catch you off guard?

_____

_____

_____

3. Is there anything you need to settle with from your childhood?

_____

_____

_____

4. Philippians 3:13-14
   Reflect on these verses. How can you start walking in them today?

_____

_____

5. Imagine forgetting or leaving the past behind. What would that look like in your life now?

_____

_____

_____

_____

6. What do you need to stop dragging along with you from the past?

_____

_____

_____

_____

COVERED

ON A DEEPER LEVEL

Chapter 2

Daddy Died

1. James 1:2-3
   Meditate on these verses. How can you start living by them today?

   _____

   _____

   _____

2. Psalm 34:8
   Reflect on this verse. How can you apply it to your life today?

   _____

   _____

   _____

3. Have you tasted God's goodness? When? In what ways?

   _____

   _____

   _____

4. What is God calling you to step out into?

   _____

   _____

   _____

5. Have you lost sight of your dreams? When? In what ways?

_____

_____

_____

_____

6. Have the circumstances of life left you wondering why you are here and what your purpose is? Explain.

_____

_____

_____

_____

COVERED

_____
_____
_____
_____
_____
_____
_____
_____
_____
_____
_____
_____
_____
_____
_____
_____
_____
_____
_____
_____
_____
_____

ON A DEEPER LEVEL

_____
_____
_____
_____
_____
_____
_____
_____
_____
_____
_____
_____
_____
_____
_____
_____
_____
_____
_____
_____
_____
_____
_____

Chapter 3

Can I Trust You?

1. What do you do when you find out someone isn't who you thought they were? And what about if that someone is your spouse or another close friend or family member?

_____

_____

_____

_____

2. Do you see an area where the enemy is trying to stop something good in your life?

_____

_____

_____

_____

3. John 1:2
   Meditate on this verse. How can you apply it today?

_____

_____

_____

_____

4. James 4:3
   Reflect on this verse. How can you start walking in this verse today?

_____

_____

_____

_____

5. Proverbs 3:6
   Ponder this verse. How will this verse change your life today?

_____

_____

_____

_____

6. In what way do you need Him to make your paths straight and smooth?

_____

_____

_____

_____

7. Are you willing to ask, listen, obey, and believe? What does that look
   like to you?

_____

_____

_____

_____

COVERED

_____
_____
_____
_____
_____
_____
_____
_____
_____
_____
_____
_____
_____
_____
_____
_____
_____
_____
_____
_____
_____
_____
_____

ON A DEEPER LEVEL

_____
_____
_____
_____
_____
_____
_____
_____
_____
_____
_____
_____
_____
_____
_____
_____
_____
_____
_____
_____
_____
_____
_____
_____
_____

Chapter 4

I Get to Live

1. Why do I get to live? Have you ever asked yourself this before? When and under what circumstances?

_____

_____

_____

2. Proverbs 3:5-6
   Reflect on these verses. How will you live by them today?

_____

_____

_____

3. What would it look like if you learned to be a flexible person?

_____

_____

_____

4. How would that change the outcome when things don't go as planned?

_____

_____

_____

5. What if you could pivot and look for new opportunities in the situation at hand? In what ways would your perspective change?

_____

_____

_____

6. What would happen if you got curious about why you're feeling a certain way or why you have what you have in your life?

_____

_____

_____

7. What would happen if you looked at your thoughts and changed them?

_____

_____

_____

8. James 4:14
   Meditate on this verse. How will you apply it to your life?

_____

_____

_____

9. 2 Chronicles 20:15
   Reflect on this verse. How will it change your life today?

_____

_____

10. James 1:2-4

You should be getting to know these verses very well by now. How are they changing your life?

_____

_____

_____

11. What will you allow the trials that you face to produce in you?

_____

_____

_____

12. What will you choose to do when you face trials of many kinds?

_____

_____

_____

13. What would happen if you allowed yourself to grow?

_____

_____

_____

14. John 15:5

Ponder this verse. How will you start walking in it today?

_____

_____

_____

15. What would it take for you to step toward living a yielded life in Christ?

_____

_____

_____

16. What thoughts would you have to think?

_____

_____

_____

17. Is your life going the way you want it to go? Or are you being shaken by every trial that comes your way?

_____

_____

_____

18. Acts 17:28
Meditate on this verse. How will it change your life starting today?

_____

_____

19. John 16:33
Reflect on this verse. What will this verse look like when applied to your life?

_____

_____

COVERED

_____
_____
_____
_____
_____
_____
_____
_____
_____
_____
_____
_____
_____
_____
_____
_____
_____
_____
_____
_____
_____
_____
_____
_____

ON A DEEPER LEVEL

_____
_____
_____
_____
_____
_____
_____
_____
_____
_____
_____
_____
_____
_____
_____
_____
_____
_____
_____
_____
_____
_____
_____
_____

Chapter 5

Overwhelmed with Three Kids

1. Psalm 127:3
   Meditate on this verse. What will this verse look like in your life today?

   _____

   _____

   _____

2. If you don't love yourself, how can you love others? Explain.

   _____

   _____

   _____

3. Matthew 22:36-39
   Reflect on these verses. How will you walk in them today?

   _____

   _____

   _____

4. James 2:8
   Meditate on this verse. How will you apply it today?

   _____

   _____

   _____

5. Will you receive this "while we were still sinners" gift and be open to His amazing, unconditional love? What does that mean to you?

_____

_____

_____

_____

6. Romans 5:8
   Ponder this verse. How will it change your life today?

_____

_____

_____

7. Isn't that amazing love? What would it look like for you to just bask in God's love?

_____

_____

_____

_____

8. James 4:8
   Meditate on this verse. How will you make it part of your life today?

_____

_____

_____

_____

9. My motto is: "I don't want to go through the same thing the same way again." Do you have a motto for your life? If you'd like, you can claim this one as your own as well.

_____

_____

_____

_____

10. What does it mean to you if you consider it pure joy as you face trials, knowing that the testing of your faith will make you mature and complete, lacking nothing?

_____

_____

_____

_____

11. James 1:2-4
These verses again. What changes are happening in your life as you apply these verses?

_____

_____

_____

COVERED

ON A DEEPER LEVEL

Chapter 6

Depressed to Blessed

1. Can your old spot be made new? What does that look like to you?

_____

_____

_____

2. What steps are you willing to take to get to a place of peace in your life?

_____

_____

_____

3. Do you realize that you have a choice on how you rise out of depression or any other negative spot? What does that choice look like for you?

_____

_____

_____

4. How will you get the results you want? What actions will you take?

_____

_____

_____

5. If you really believe that the Word of God is true, then you can expect
   to get results in your everyday when you apply it to your life. Does this
   ring true with you? How?

   _____

   _____

   _____

6. Hebrews 4:12
   Meditate on this verse. How will you start walking in it?

   _____

   _____

   _____

7. Mark 11:25
   Reflect on this verse. What will you do to walk this verse out?

   _____

   _____

   _____

8. Psalm 118:24
   Meditate on this verse. Is this verse true in your life?

   _____

   _____

   _____

9. Do you need to renew your mind with this verse? In what areas?

   _____

   _____

   _____

10. Have you been struggling with depression, fear, anxiety, or overwhelm?

_____

_____

11. How will believing and doing this verse change your life?

_____

_____

_____

12. Hebrews 11:6
Ponder this verse. What will this verse look like in your life when you apply it?

_____

_____

_____

13. Numbers 6:24-26
Meditate on these verses. Will you start speaking and picturing this blessing over you and yours?

_____

_____

_____

14. Do you believe the Word so much, that you see the need for it to go before you and your family?

_____

_____

_____

15. Does this idea of blessing your family stir up anything in you? Write that down here.

_____

_____

_____

_____

16. Does it feel uncomfortable? Will they think you are crazy? Why would you let "uncomfortable" make your decision for you? Explain.

_____

_____

_____

_____

17. What scriptures do you need to apply to your life and family?

_____

_____

_____

_____

COVERED

ON A DEEPER LEVEL

_____

_____

_____

_____

_____

_____

_____

_____

_____

_____

_____

_____

_____

_____

_____

_____

_____

_____

_____

_____

_____

Chapter 7

Full Days, Lessons Learned

1. Romans 8:14
   Meditate on this verse. Are you walking this verse out in your life?

   _____

   _____

2. Why are you trying to figure _____ out? Why are you not believing
   that you are led in _____ area? Fill in the blanks by using the space
   below.

   _____

   _____

   _____

3. Do you need to change your thoughts about _____ to a thanksgiving
   prayer? Write about it down below.

   _____

   _____

   _____

4. Isaiah 54:13
   Reflect on this verse. What if you believed this verse for your life?

   _____

   _____

5. Ephesians 3:20-21
   Meditate on these verses. How will your life change if you believe these verses and walk in them?

   _____

   _____

   _____

6. Assuming you consider yourself a believer. What will your life look like if you step into another level of acting like one?

   _____

   _____

7. 1 Peter 5:7
   Reflect on this verse. Are you doing this verse in your life yet?

   _____

   _____

8. James 1:6-8
   Meditate on these verses. What will it take for you to start walking out these verses in your life?

   _____

   _____

9. John 6:28-29
   Ponder these verses. What is our work as Christians?

   _____

   _____

   _____

10. As a Christian, if you are not believing the Word, why do you even bother with God or the Bible at all?

_____

_____

_____

11. Revelation 3:16
Meditate on this verse. Do you want to be spiritually useless?

_____

_____

_____

12. Why would you do something and only do it halfway?

_____

_____

_____

13. Believe God. How do you see things working out if you don't?

_____

_____

_____

14. How will you get to the point where you are on fire for Him and the assignment He has put you in charge of?

_____

_____

_____

15. Psalm 127:1
Reflect on this verse. What do you need to let the Lord build in your life?

_____

_____

16. Proverbs 3:6
Meditate on this verse. How will you start walking in the light of this verse today?

_____

_____

17. Matthew 16:5
Ponder this verse. What will it look like for you to walk out this verse starting today?

_____

_____

18. Will you stop doing things in vain? When will you be willing to change?

_____

_____

19. What do you need to let go of in your life, your marriage, your family, your home, or your business? Letting go will be uncomfortable, are you ready for that?

_____

_____

_____

20. Is it working the way you have been doing it?

_____

_____

_____

21. What are you trying to control? Do you realize the harder you hold on the quicker it slips out of your hands?

_____

_____

_____

22. Joshua 1:8
Meditate on this verse. What would it look like if you lived this verse out in your life?

_____

_____

_____

23. Romans 8:28
Reflect on this verse. What will your life look like if you believe this verse?

_____

_____

_____

24. Why would you question God's goodness? In what situations do you?

_____

_____

_____

COVERED

ON A DEEPER LEVEL

Chapter 8

There Must Be More

1. Matthew 5:6
   Meditate on this verse. Is this verse true of you?

   _____

   _____

   _____

2. Ephesians 5:18
   Reflect on this verse. How will you live by this scripture?

   _____

   _____

   _____

3. Hebrews 12:1
   Meditate on this verse. What if you did what this verse is saying?

   _____

   _____

   _____

4. 1 Peter 2:9
   Ponder this verse. What if you walk in this identity?

   _____

   _____

   _____

5. If the word is true and I'm a believer, I will believe the word and see the results of it. There is no room for any other option in my life. Either I believe the word, or I don't. Either I act like a believer, or I don't. Either the word is true or it's not. And if it isn't true, then why waste my time on it? Will you settle this in your own heart? What does this mean to you?

_____

_____

_____

_____

6. Matthew 7:7-8, 11
   Meditate on these verses. How will you live by these verses today?

_____

_____

_____

7. Luke 11:13
   Reflect on this verse. Will you walk in this verse today?

_____

_____

_____

8. Why wouldn't we, as believers, be happy when God is leading our fellow Christians to a different spot? Could that new spot mean growth and direction for them from God?

_____

_____

_____

9. Why do we judge and fear the steps of other believers? Would God be telling you what other Christians are supposed to do?

_____

_____

_____

_____

10. Why do we go against other believers when someone leaves their local body for another one? Aren't we all a part of one Body, the Body of Christ, one Church?

_____

_____

_____

_____

COVERED

_____

_____

_____

_____

_____

_____

_____

_____

_____

_____

_____

_____

_____

_____

_____

_____

_____

_____

_____

_____

_____

_____

_____

_____

ON A DEEPER LEVEL

Chapter 9

Pack My Bags?

1. Psalm 91:2
   Meditate on this verse. Will you believe this is who He is for you?

   _____

   _____

   _____

2. Proverbs 18:10
   Reflect on this verse. What will your life look like if you believe this?

   _____

   _____

3. The Lord told me to "pack my bags." What is He telling you to do that you simply need to obey?

   _____

   _____

   _____

4. Ask yourself: Is what I have been taught, or is it just what my parents were taught or what the church I grew up in taught? Explain.

   _____

   _____

   _____

5. Mark 7:8.
   Meditate on this verse. Where are you at in regard to this verse?

   _____

   _____

   _____

6. Is that what most of us have been doing for years—just walking in the tradition of men? Write your answer below.

   _____

   _____

   _____

7. Are traditions of men why we haven't got the results in our lives we are longing for?

   _____

   _____

8. Many of the ways we have been taught are just reasonable, sensible, or even religious. Is that the God of the Bible? Yes or no? Explain your answer below.

   _____

   _____

   _____

9. Look at the stories of Abraham, Moses, and Noah. Does what God asked them to do line up with our religious teaching or natural mind?

   _____

   _____

10. Do you think God will ask you to do only the ordinary thing? Why?

_____

_____

11. Do you think He will ask you to do only the things that everyone agrees with? Explain.

_____

_____

12. How many impossible things have you done in your lifetime? List a few below.

_____

_____

_____

13. If your daily life doesn't require God, are you living big enough?

_____

_____

14. Luke 1:37
Ponder this verse. How are you applying this verse to your life?

_____

_____

_____

15. Will you believe Him and obey Him? How?

_____

_____

16. Will you step out and make the uncomfortable choice in your impossible situation? How?

_____

_____

17. It was scary to think what packing my bags might lead to. But did I really know what it might lead to? Answer below.

_____

_____

_____

18. What is simple obedience to you?

_____

_____

_____

19. 1 Samuel 15:22
Meditate on this verse. What will this verse look like in your life?

_____

_____

_____

20. Romans 8:28
Reflect on this verse. What will be different in your life if you believe this verse?

_____

_____

_____

21. Will you choose to believe ALL things work out for your good?

_____

_____

22. Do you want your life to stay just the way it is or do you want to live the extraordinary, impossible life God has for you? How will your life change?

_____

_____

23. What are you trying to save by doing nothing? Do you think you are keeping everyone safe? Why?

_____

_____

_____

24. Do you want your marriage or other areas of your life to stay in an unhealthy place?

_____

_____

_____

25. What are you saying to your kids or others (that look up to you) if you stay in that unhealthy place? Why?

_____

_____

_____

26. Why don't you be the one to turn the situation around with God's guidance? Is this something you see yourself capable of? What's stopping you?

_____

_____

_____

27. Has the attitude, issue, or problem been in your family for generations? Why don't you be the one to take a step toward change?

_____

_____

_____

28. What if that step changed everything for future generations? Explain the effects it would have.

_____

_____

_____

29. What is your next step to shift the seemingly impossible situation or circumstance in your life?

_____

_____

_____

30. He works out all things for the good of those who love Him...do you love Him? Is He your first love?

_____

_____

COVERED

_____

_____

_____

_____

_____

_____

_____

_____

_____

_____

_____

_____

_____

_____

_____

_____

_____

_____

_____

_____

_____

_____

_____

ON A DEEPER LEVEL

Chapter 10

On the Verge of a Grand Mal Seizure

1. Colossians 3:4
   Meditate on this verse. How will your life look if you follow this verse?

   _____

   _____

2. Romans 8:14
   Reflect on this verse. How will your life change if you believe this verse?

   _____

   _____

3. Do you have the negative thoughts that continually swirl around in your mind? How long can this keep happening before there are negative side effects?

   _____

   _____

4. How often do you go over and over thoughts in your mind, trying to figure things out, trying to see where you went wrong, or blaming the other person--only to end up in the same spot?

   _____

   _____

5. Isaiah 54:17
   Meditate on this verse. How will you apply this verse to your life?

_____

_____

_____

6. Isaiah 53:5
   Ponder this verse. What will your life look like if you believe this verse?

_____

_____

_____

7. 1 Corinthians 14:2
   Meditate on this verse. How will you walk it out?

_____

_____

_____

8. 1 Corinthians 14:4
   Reflect on this verse. How will you apply this verse to your life?

_____

_____

_____

9. Jude 1:20
   Meditate on this verse. How will belief in this verse change your life?

_____

_____

_____

10. If you don't believe or have faith in healing, do you think you will see it happen in your life? Explain.

_____

_____

_____

11. Hebrews 6:12
Ponder this verse. How will your life change if you believe it?

_____

_____

12. Psalm 103:2-3
Meditate on these verses. How do these verses apply to you?

_____

_____

13. Do you believe God will heal when you ask Him to? Do you have the faith for healing?

_____

_____

_____

14. Do you physically see forgiveness of sin, or do you simply believe it by faith? Isn't it the same idea with healing?

_____

_____

_____

15. Luke 8:48
Reflect on this verse. How will belief in this verse change your life?

_____

_____

_____

16. Let's pray simple prayers of belief. Does it have to be complicated? Write a simple prayer of belief down here.

_____

_____

_____

17. John 6:28-29
Meditate on these verses. How will applying these verses to your life change it?

_____

_____

_____

18. John 1:1, 14
Ponder these verses. Do you believe them?

_____

_____

_____

19. Simply, what is your work as a Christian?

_____

_____

_____

20. 1 John 3:1

Meditate on this verse. How will belief in this verse transform your life?

_____

_____

_____

21. Are you ready to receive the Father's amazing love? Tell Him you receive it now.

_____

_____

_____

22. Will you let Him into every area? Open completely to Him now.

_____

_____

_____

23. Will you believe you are healed? Write a prayer of belief here.

_____

_____

_____

COVERED

ON A DEEPER LEVEL

Chapter 11

Stripped of Who I Was

1. Why keep interacting in the same unhealthy ways? What does it benefit you?

_____

_____

_____

2. Psalm 147:3
   Meditate on this verse. Will you receive this verse for your life?

_____

_____

3. Romans 12:19
   Reflect on this verse. Will you believe this and allow it to change your life?

_____

_____

4. What does "I WILL REPAY," says the LORD mean to you?

_____

_____

5. Write out a prayer for your "enemy". You can change the one I prayed to fit your situation (from page 137 in the book).

_____

_____

_____

_____

_____

_____

_____

_____

6. Is there an area in your life you need to step out of? How will that look?

_____

_____

_____

7. What do you need to change?

_____

_____

_____

8. What if changing yourself is key? Change what you are thinking about the situation. Write your thoughts down below.

_____

_____

_____

9. What if your children and others see you take a stand against unrighteousness? How will that effect them and you?

_____

_____

_____

10. What will happen if they see you speak up and use your voice?

_____

_____

_____

11. Could this keep them from having the same troubles in their lives? Explain your answer.

_____

_____

_____

12. Is it worth changing in a positive way for the generations ahead? Explain.

_____

_____

_____

13. Isn't it worth being uncomfortable for a little while to bring about right relationships in the future? Write your thoughts.

_____

_____

_____

COVERED

ON A DEEPER LEVEL

_____

_____

_____

_____

_____

_____

_____

_____

_____

_____

_____

_____

_____

_____

_____

_____

_____

_____

_____

_____

_____

_____

Chapter 12

Back to School

1. Ephesians 3:20
   Meditate on this verse. Will you believe this verse and walk in it?

   _____

   _____

2. Matthew 19:26
   Reflect on this verse. What would your life look like if you believe this verse?

   _____

   _____

3. Philippians 1:21
   Meditate on this verse. How will belief in this verse change your life?

   _____

   _____

   _____

4. What is the difference between the words surrendered and yielded? Look them up and write your answers below.

   _____

   _____

   _____

5. How will you live in relation to God?

_____

_____

_____

6. Colossians 3:4
   Ponder this verse. What does this verse mean to you?

_____

_____

_____

7. 1 Corinthians 6:20
   Meditate on this verse. If this verse is true, how will you live according to it?

_____

_____

_____

8. Romans 6:11
   Reflect on this verse. How will you live different in light of this verse?

_____

_____

_____

9. Is there an area in your life you keep agreeing to that you need to speak up about? What is it and what is God saying about it?

_____

_____

_____

10. Isaiah 1:19
Meditate on this verse. How are you lining up with this Word today?

_____

_____

_____

11. Would you consider yourself in the category of willing and obedient? If not, why not?

_____

_____

_____

12. Do you think it will work out for you any other way? Explain.

_____

_____

_____

COVERED

ON A DEEPER LEVEL

Chapter 13

Willing to Receive Gifts
From God

1. Is there an area you are resisting moving forward in out of fear? What is it?

_____

_____

2. Do you think you know better than God?

_____

_____

3. What if you step into the next place and it takes God to make it happen? How does this change your outlook on the situation?

_____

_____

_____

4. Shouldn't your daily life take faith? If it doesn't, are you living big enough?

_____

_____

_____

5. Where are you at? Are you living safe, comfortable, and easy when God is bidding you to let go of the physical securities and take a risk or step out on the water where there is nothing physical to hang on to?

_____

_____

_____

6. Hebrews 12:2
   Meditate on this verse. How will belief in this verse change your life?

_____

_____

_____

7. Hebrews 11:6
   Reflect on this verse. How will you apply this verse to your life today?

_____

_____

_____

8. Romans 8:28
   Meditate on this verse. How will you line up with this verse today?

_____

_____

_____

9. Are you willing to say yes to the extravagant gifts He wants to bless you with?

_____

_____

10. Will you be more aware of what God wants for you rather than insisting on your own way? Explain.

_____

_____

_____

11. Considering all that we've talked about, oh what He will do for you if you believe. Will you believe?

_____

_____

_____

COVERED

ON A DEEPER LEVEL

_____

_____

_____

_____

_____

_____

_____

_____

_____

_____

_____

_____

_____

_____

_____

_____

_____

_____

_____

Chapter 14

Become a Covenant Life Coach?

1. Imagine… an unstable dock and nothing physical to hang on to. What if this feeling of instability (uncomfortableness) became your new normal?

   _____

   _____

2. Matthew 14:29
   Meditate on this verse. How will you walk in this verse today?

   _____

   _____

   _____

3. Matthew 7:24-27
   Reflect on these verses. How will you apply this to your life?

   _____

   _____

   _____

4. Psalm 62:6
   Meditate on this verse. What will your life look like if you walk out this verse today?

   _____

   _____

5. Are you obeying money or God? What if you make obeying God the only option?

_____

_____

_____

6. Are you willing to put your treasure where your heart is? In what area is God asking you to do this?

_____

_____

_____

7. Matthew 6:21
Ponder this verse. How is God leading you to apply this verse to your life today?

_____

_____

_____

8. Is getting out of debt the focus God wants you to have?

_____

_____

_____

9. Read and meditate on 2 Kings 4, the story about Elisha and the woman's oil. Did Elisha tell her to start a business?

_____

_____

10. Take some time to look into what the Bible says about money and business. Write three verses you found on the subject.

_____

_____

_____

11. Will you be willing to stop playing it safe? Explain.

_____

_____

_____

12. Will you do the thing that makes you feel sick to your stomach, or will you choose to stay comfortable? Write your answer below.

_____

_____

_____

13. Matthew 7:14
    Meditate on this verse. How will believing this truth change your life?

_____

_____

_____

14. Ephesians 6:19-20
    Reflect on these verses. How does God want you to apply this verse today?

_____

_____

15. Romans 6:18
    Meditate on this verse. Who are you according to this verse?

    _____

    _____

    _____

16. Philippians 3:20
    Ponder this verse. How will you live different if you believe it?

    _____

    _____

    _____

17. Matthew 6:33
    Meditate on this verse. How will you live different knowing this verse?

    _____

    _____

    _____

18. Do you have inner peace and direction from the Lord when you walk
    by faith? Is it easy?

    _____

    _____

    _____

19. Hebrews 12:1-2
    Reflect on these verses. How do these verses apply to your life?

    _____

    _____

20. Will you endure until the end, take the narrow path, and throw off the weights that are entangling you? Answer below.

_____

_____

_____

21. Will you forget the past so you can reach toward the goal of the high call of God? How?

_____

_____

_____

22. Philippians 3:13-14
Meditate on this verse. How will it change your life today?

_____

_____

_____

23. How will you show yourself worthy of your race and your call?

_____

_____

_____

24. What does "few are chosen" mean?

_____

_____

_____

25. What is the call? Are you too busy to answer the call?

_____

_____

_____

26. Matthew 10:39
Ponder this verse. What does it mean for you?

_____

_____

_____

27. 1 Corinthians 6:20
Meditate on this verse. How will you walk in this verse today?

_____

_____

_____

28. As part of the Body of Christ, part of the Church, what are you waiting for? Do you believe you are the move of God?

_____

_____

_____

_____

29. What is God calling you to do?

_____

_____

_____

30. Have you considered investing in your future by hiring a coach, not just any life coach, but a Covenant Life Coach, who is in relationship with the Spirit of God?

_____

_____

_____

_____

_____

_____

_____

_____

COVERED

_____

_____

_____

_____

_____

_____

_____

_____

_____

_____

_____

_____

_____

_____

_____

_____

_____

_____

_____

_____

_____

_____

_____

ON A DEEPER LEVEL

Conclusion

1. Where are you in your spiritual journey, starting your walk of faith, continuing your walk of faith, or ready to take your life of faith to the next level?

_____

_____

_____

_____

2. What is your next step?

_____

_____

_____

_____

3. What weights do you need to throw off so you can run your race?

_____

_____

_____

_____

4. What if you believed you are COVERED?

_____

_____

_____

5. What could your life look like if you believed the Word over your circumstances?

_____

_____

_____

_____

6. What would it look like for you to start walking in the goodness and fullness of God?

_____

_____

_____

_____

7. What would it look like if you started believing in healing?

_____

_____

_____

_____

8. What if belief in and speaking His name started changing your circumstances? What would that mean in your life?

_____

_____

_____

_____

9. What if you started thinking or believing something different? How would your life change?

_____

_____

_____

_____

10. What if you believed you didn't have to be broke or live paycheck to paycheck? How would your finances change?

_____

_____

_____

_____

11. What if what got you here won't get you there? What different step do you need to take to go toward your next place?

_____

_____

_____

_____

12. What if you have to think differently to get the results you want? Explain.

_____

_____

_____

_____

13. What if you let yourself dream again? What would that look like?

_____

_____

_____

14. What could that make possible?

_____

_____

_____

15. Proverbs 23:7
    Meditate on this verse. What will you do in light of it?

_____

_____

_____

16. Romans 12:2
    Reflect on this verse. How will you apply this verse to your life?

_____

_____

_____

17. Proverbs 18:10
    Meditate on this verse. How will this verse change your life?

_____

_____

_____

18. Psalm 91:2
    Ponder this verse. Knowing this verse, how will it change your life?

    _____

    _____

    _____

19. 1 John 1:7
    Meditate on this verse. How will you walk in it today?

    _____

    _____

20. Can you picture yourself COVERED and live COVERED in every
    area?

    _____

    _____

    _____

21. Colossians 3:3
    Reflect on this verse. Is belief in this verse going to bring about life
    change?

    _____

    _____

    _____

22. 2 Corinthians 2:14
    Meditate on this verse. Who are you according to this verse?

    _____

    _____

23. What if sharing your story will make a difference in the world? What does that statement bring about inside of you?

_____

_____

_____

_____

24. Be sure to take some time saying confessions over your life and family. Use mine in the Appendix at the back of the book COVERED Living in triumph while going through trials.

_____

_____

_____

_____

_____

_____

_____

_____

Congratulations! You did it!
Next Step?
Join one on one or group coaching.
Contact Jackie for details.

COVERED

ON A DEEPER LEVEL

About the Author

Jackie Dighans is a daughter of God Most High. She has been married to her husband, Justin, for twenty-nine years. Together, they have ten children (yes, they are all biological; no, there are not any twins). The children range from seven to twenty-six years old. They have three married children and four grandchildren. Six children are still in the home, attending public school, and one is single, taking the next steps, while working in the family business. Jackie lives with her family in rural southeastern Montana. Jackie was a homeschool mom for almost twenty years. She attended three years of Bible school and has a certificate in Biblical Studies. Jackie is a Covenant Life Coach. She enjoys speaking at women's events, conferences, retreats, and other services. Jackie helps people come in alignment with the Covenant of God so they can live the full lives He has planned for them. She helps people throw off the weights and sin that entangle them and forget the past so they can run their race and reach the goal of the high call of God.

Author's Services

As a Covenant Life Coach, she offers one-on-one and group coaching.

Ask for details about COVERED Group Coaching.

Jackie Dighans is a public speaker. She enjoys speaking at retreats, women's events, conferences, and other services.

Contact her at jackiedighans@gmail.com.

You can also find her on Facebook, Instagram, TikTok, and YouTube at Jackie Dighans.

Her podcast called Dripping with Abundance is on Spotify.

This bonus material was created to accompany Jackie's book COVERED Living in triumph while going through trials.

Watch for Jackie's second book,
WHAT IF YOU BELIEVED? 31 Beliefs to Act on From the Living Word to Bring About Life Change.

www.ingramcontent.com/pod-product-compliance
Lightning Source LLC
Chambersburg PA
CBHW021004150626
46549CB00012BA/1056